RACIAL JUSTICE IN AM...
INDIGENOUS PEOPLES

LONGHOUSE FORM OF GOVERNMENT

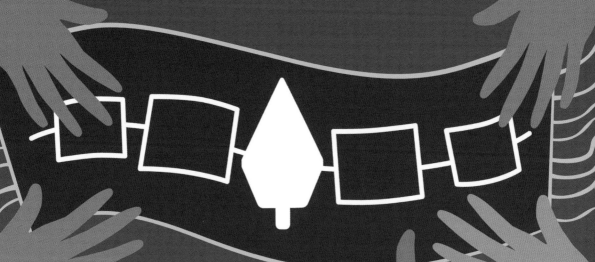

HEATHER BRUEGL

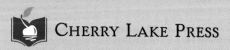
CHERRY LAKE PRESS

Published in the United States of America by Cherry Lake Publishing Group
Ann Arbor, Michigan
www.cherrylakepublishing.com

Reading Adviser: Beth Walker Gambro, MS, Ed., Reading Consultant, Yorkville, IL
Cover Art: Felicia Macheske

Produced by Focus Strategic Communications Inc.

Photo Credits: © Brett Zimmerman/Shutterstock, 5; © fandangle/Shutterstock, 7; © EWY Media/Shutterstock, 9; Onondaga Nation, Six Nations Legacy Consortium Collection, Six Nations Public Library, 11; National Portrait Gallery, Smithsonian Institution, 13; © Orhan Cam/Shutterstock, 14; Photo by Jeff Reed, National Archives, 17; Architect of the Capitol via Wikimedia Commons, 18, 19; National Portrait Gallery, Smithsonian Institution via Wikimedia Commons, 21; © Richard Laschon/Shutterstock, 21 (inset); UK Parliament via Wikimedia Commons, Attribution 3.0 Unported, 25; © Frank L Junior/Shutterstock, 26; © Jakub Zajic/Shutterstock, 27; © Gregory Johnston/Shutterstock, 29; Library of Congress, 31

Cherry Lake Press is an imprint of Cherry Lake Publishing Group.

Library of Congress Cataloging-in-Publication Data

Names: Bruegl, Heather, author.
Title: Longhouse form of government / Heather Bruegl.
Description: Ann Arbor, MI : Cherry Lake Publishing, [2024]. | Series: Racial justice in America: Indigenous peoples | Audience: Grades 7-9 | Summary: "Indigenous nations have always been political bodies. In this book, readers will learn how the longhouse form of government worked, the peoples that used it, and the influence it had on U.S. history and politics. Through these influences, readers are invited to celebrate Indigenous achievements and excellence in governing. The Racial Justice in America: Indigenous Peoples series explores the issues specific to the Indigenous communities in the United States in a comprehensive, honest, and age-appropriate way. This series was written by Indigenous historian and public scholar Heather Bruegl, a citizen of the Oneida Nation of Wisconsin and a first-line descendant Stockbridge Munsee. The series was developed to reach children of all races and encourage them to approach race, diversity, and inclusion with open eyes and minds"— Provided by publisher.
Identifiers: LCCN 2023043602 | ISBN 9781668937969 (hardcover) | ISBN 9781668939000 (paperback) | ISBN 9781668940341 (ebook) | ISBN 9781668941690 (pdf)
Subjects: LCSH: Five Nations—History—Juvenile literature. | Indians of North America—New York (State)—Politics and government—Juvenile literature.
Classification: LCC E98.T77 B77 2024 | DDC 320.089970747—dc23/eng/20231012
LC record available at https://lccn.loc.gov/2023043602

Cherry Lake Publishing would like to acknowledge the work of the Partnership for 21st Century Learning, a Network of Battelle for Kids. Please visit Battelle for Kids online for more information.

Printed in the United States of America

Note from publisher: Websites change regularly, and their future contents are outside of our control. Supervise children when conducting any recommended online searches for extended learning opportunities.

Heather Bruegl, Oneida Nation of Wisconsin/Stockbridge-Munsee is a Madonna University graduate with a Master of Arts in U.S. History. Heather is a public historian and decolonial educator and travels frequently to present on Indigenous history, including policy and activism. In the Munsee language, Heather's name is Kiishookunkwe, meaning sunflower in full bloom.

CHAPTER 1

The Haudenosaunee

Indigenous peoples were the first peoples to live on the land that is now part of the United States. Indigenous groups were not just cultural groups. They were also political nations that had distinct governments. These nations had trade agreements and **allies**. They sometimes had enemies, too.

In the Northeast, five Indigenous nations agreed to work together. They formed a **confederacy** called the Five Nations. This group was also called the **Haudenosaunee**, or the "People of the Longhouse."

Extended families lived together in Haudenosaunee longhouses.

These nations lived in what is now the state of New York. The Five Nations included the Mohawk, Oneida, Onondaga, Cayuga, and Seneca peoples. This confederacy did more than just ensure peace. It later influenced the creation of the United States government.

The Haudenosaunee was founded in the year 1142. We have learned from Haudenosaunee members about this time in their history. The Five Nations had been battling each other, and the cost of war was high. People demanded peace.

A leader called the Great Peacemaker arrived and brought harmony to the Five Nations. His name was Tekanawí:ta. Some retellings say he was a Huron, while others say he was born an Onondaga but later adopted by the Mohawk.

The Great Peacemaker traveled across all five warring nations, bringing a message of peace. Hiawatha, who was Onondaga, traveled with him and spoke the Great Peacemaker's message.

The original five nations of the Haudenosaunee Confederacy are represented by five symbols: four boxes and the Great Tree of Peace.

After the meetings, a great council was called. The Great Law of Peace was presented to the Haudenosaunee. The Great Law of Peace became the confederacy's constitution. Each nation would maintain its leadership. They formed a General Council to decide together on common issues.

The Great Law of Peace was recorded on **wampum belts**. These belts were handed down by the Great Peacemaker. The Great Law was spoken by Hiawatha. After the law was spoken, a large white pine was uprooted from the ground. The items of war from all five peoples were buried in the hole left behind. The tree was replaced and the peace was sealed.

For hundreds of years, the Haudenosaunee Confederacy was strong. The Tuscarora Nation joined it, making it the Six Nations. Other nations joined it as well. Europeans who later arrived allied themselves with the Haudenosaunee, as they offered protection, trade, and knowledge.

The Haudenosaunee Confederacy was **matrilineal**.
Clan membership was passed down through mothers'
lines and the clan mothers had a lot of political power.
The French and the British didn't understand this.
They were used to only men being in charge.

Wampum belts held messages and recorded oaths and treaties.

The American Revolution divided the Haudenosaunee and broke the Great Peace. Different nations now fought on different sides. After the war, they signed separate treaties.

The Tuscarora and the Oneida fought with the United States. Other nations remaining in New York were forced to give up their lands. The Tuscarora and Oneida were given more land. They were also given money for education and the construction of a sawmill. The Mohawk sided with the British. They received a land grant in Canada and formed their own confederacy there instead.

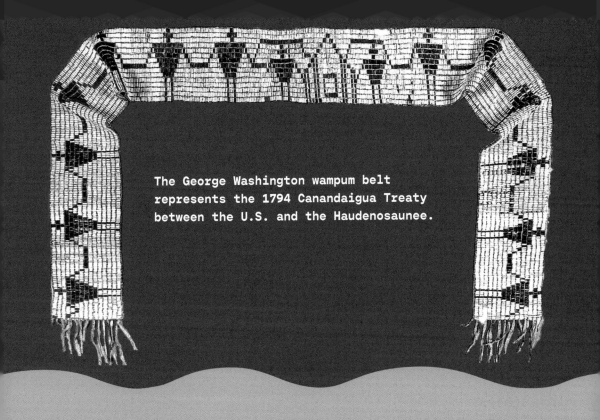

The George Washington wampum belt represents the 1794 Canandaigua Treaty between the U.S. and the Haudenosaunee.

The five original Haudenosaunee nations:

- Mohawk—Kanien'kehá:ka, People of the Flint
- Oneida—Onayotekaono, People of the Standing Stone
- Onondaga—Onundagaono, People of the Hills
- Cayuga—Guyohkohnyoh, People of the Great Swamp
- Seneca—Onondowahgah, People of the Great Hill

CHAPTER 2

The Constitution of the United States

The United States gained its independence from Great Britain in 1776 and needed to set up its own government. The new government needed a set of laws to guide it. The first was the Articles of Confederation, but this set of laws did not work out. The Constitution of the United States was signed on September 17, 1787, in Philadelphia, Pennsylvania. The Constitution was the second set of laws governing the new United States.

Leaders of the states held a Constitutional Convention in Philadelphia. Delegates from 12 states attended. Rhode Island did not send any delegates because it did not want a stronger central government.

James Madison visited the Haudenosaunee in 1784.

The delegates in attendance became known as the Framers of the Constitution. One delegate, James Madison, is known as the Father of the Constitution. The delegates met in secret. News reporters and visitors were not allowed to enter these convention meetings. Madison took detailed notes throughout the convention, documenting who spoke and describing their arguments.

The United States Capitol Building is where both houses of Congress work.

After months of debate, a final document was created. It divided the government into three branches: the legislature, the executive, and the judiciary. Each branch had powers that the other two did not, which created a system of checks and balances.

The document also described how states would be represented. The Connecticut Compromise created two houses of Congress. The House of Representatives would have representatives based on population. The Senate would have two representatives from each state, no matter what the population was. The delegates hoped this would allow smaller states to still have a strong voice in Congress.

The final document contained around 4,200 words. On September 17, 1787, George Washington was the first to sign the Constitution of the United States. In order for the U.S. Constitution to become law, though, nine of the thirteen states would need to officially adopt it. Alexander Hamilton, James Madison, and John Jay wrote essays called *The Federalist Papers* to convince people to accept it.

Starting on December 7 of the same year, five states ratified the document: Delaware, Pennsylvania, New Jersey, Georgia, and Connecticut. Massachusetts and other states withheld ratifying the U.S. Constitution because they wanted to ensure fundamental rights were protected. By February 1788, a compromise was reached with the promise that amendments would be added. These first 10 amendments are known as the Bill of Rights.

Massachusetts, Maryland, South Carolina, and New Hampshire were next to ratify the U.S. Constitution, thus making it law. On April 30, 1789, Washington was sworn in as the first president of the United States. In June of 1789, Virginia ratified the U.S. Constitution, and New York followed in July. The Supreme Court opened on February 2, 1790, making the new government fully functional. Rhode Island finally ratified the U.S. Constitution on May 29, 1790.

The original Constitution of the United States is on display in the Rotunda of the National Archives building in Washington, D.C.

The delegates who attended the Constitutional Convention included many of the most influential leaders of the young nation. Some had served in the Continental Congress during the American Revolution. Six delegates had also signed the Declaration of Independence:

George Clymer
Benjamin Franklin

Robert Morris
George Read

Roger Sherman
James Wilson

This painting shows the delegates at the Constitutional Convention, with George Washington leading it on the right.

Five delegates had also signed the Articles of Confederation:

John Dickinson   Gouverneur Morris   Roger Sherman
Daniel Carroll   Robert Morris

The nation's first president, George Washington, and its first Secretary of the Treasury, Alexander Hamilton, were also delegates at the Constitutional Convention.

CHAPTER 3

How Are the Governments the Same?

So how did the Haudenosaunee influence the U.S. Constitution? In 1744, Canassatego, an Onondaga leader, gave a speech at the Treaty of Lancaster. He urged the 13 colonies to unite as the Haudenosaunee had. Benjamin Franklin printed this treaty, and he was inspired by Canassatego's words.

In his speech, Canassatego said that the colonies should unite and come to an agreement. He explained the origins of the Haudenosaunee and how this unity made them stronger and important in the region. He used a metaphor that many arrows cannot be as easily broken as one. This metaphor inspired the bundle of 13 arrows in the Great Seal of the United States.

E PLURIBUS UNUM

13
Arrows

Benjamin Franklin was a scholar, diplomat, inventor, and writer.

The Founding Fathers, including Franklin, were in regular contact with the Haudenosaunee. When Franklin presented the Albany Plan of Union in 1754, he referenced the Haudenosaunee Confederacy. The Albany Plan of Union was a plan to create a united government for the 13 colonies.

Benjamin Franklin printed this political cartoon in *The Pennsylvania Gazette* on May 9, 1754, to encourage Americans to join the Albany Plan. The letters stand for Georgia, South Carolina, North Carolina, Virginia, Maryland, Pennsylvania, New Jersey, New York, and New England.

Franklin spent a lot of time observing the workings of the Haudenosaunee. The Haudenosaunee Confederacy worked because it was fair and made sure that decisions were made with seven generations in mind. This meant that decisions should be made for long-term benefit. Many council chiefs were invited to speak to the Continental Congress in 1776.

The Haudenosaunee Confederacy was in no way an exact model for the U.S. Constitution. European governments also influenced the new government, especially the British Parliament. The Haudenosaunee, however, provided real-life examples of structures and laws that worked. For example, the Haudenosaunee restricts members from holding more than one office in the Confederacy. The same concept appears in Article I, Section 6, Clause 2 of the U.S. Constitution, preventing people from holding offices in more than one branch of government.

Both the Haudenosaunee Confederacy and the U.S. Constitution established a process to remove leaders, too. Article II, Section 4 of the U.S. Constitution describes how and when a leader can be impeached.

Also, the Haudenosaunee designated two branches of legislature with procedures for passing laws. Likewise, Article I, Section 1 in the U.S. Constitution, also known as the Vesting Clause, reads, "All legislative Powers herein granted shall be vested in a Congress of the United States, which shall consist of a Senate and House of Representatives." It goes on to outline their legislative powers.

The Haudenosaunee Confederacy identified who could declare war, as well. Article I, Section 8, Clause 11 of the U.S. Constitution, also known as the War Powers Clause, gives Congress a comparable power "to declare War, grant Letters of Marque and Reprisal, and make Rules concerning Captures on Land and Water."

The British House of Commons in London, England.

The British Parliament also has two houses of government—the House of Commons and the House of Lords. Members of the House of Commons are elected, and there are 650 members. Members of the House of Lords are appointed, and there are 781 members.

John Adams, a founder of the United States, studied European democracies. He wrote about them in *A Defense of the Constitutions of Government of the United States of America*, which was published in 1787. In it, he discusses over forty different governments, including ancient governments of Greece and Rome. The work also includes discussions of governments in England, Poland, and Switzerland, among others. Adams argued for democracy and a balance of power.

Finally, the Haudenosaunee created a balance of power between the Confederacy as a whole and individual Indigenous groups. Similarly, the 10th Amendment to the U.S. Constitution specifies that any powers not granted to the federal government belong to individual states.

The back of the 2010 Sacagawea $1 U.S. coin honors the Haudenosaunee Confederacy and the Great Law of Peace.

The *Statue of Freedom* that sits at the top of the Capitol Building's dome mixes European and Indigenous symbols, including a feathered headdress in the Haudenosaunee style.

CHAPTER 4

Are Indigenous Peoples in the U.S. Constitution?

The United States government was influenced by Indigenous peoples. The same government excluded those people as citizens. In fact, Indigenous people are only mentioned three times in the entire U.S. Constitution.

The first mention is in Article I, Section 2, Clause 3. It states, "Representatives and direct Taxes shall be apportioned among the several States . . . excluding Indians not taxed." Article I, Section 8 of the U.S. Constitution states, "Congress shall have the power to regulate Commerce with foreign nations and among the several states, and with the Indian tribes." This section implies that Indigenous nations are separate and sovereign.

Throughout U.S. history, Indigenous peoples have contributed greatly to the strength of this nation.

The final mention of Indigenous peoples is in the 14th Amendment, which reiterates Article 1, Section 2. The phrase "Indians not taxed" did not imply that Indigenous peoples did not have to pay taxes. Rather, this phrase refers to Indigenous peoples living on tribal lands. The U.S. Constitution makes a point not to count them as American citizens.

The U.S. Constitution did not govern Indigenous peoples because they were not viewed as citizens of the United States. When the 14th Amendment was passed during Reconstruction, it rightly granted citizenship to formerly enslaved peoples. It still did not, however, make Indigenous people citizens. The 15th Amendment gave those formerly enslaved males who were now citizens the right to vote. It did not grant the same right to Indigenous peoples, though.

Indigenous peoples have been outside the words of the U.S. Constitution from the beginning. But it is important to remember that Indigenous nations are sovereign nations. They have their own forms of government, leadership, and courts.

This mural by Onondaga Nation artist Brandon Lazore honors the Cayuga Indians and the greater Haudenosaunee Confederacy.

Today, there is a unique relationship between Indigenous peoples and the United States. Indigenous peoples were here first, and their governments, structures, and values helped shape this country. And yet, it was this very same country that tried to drive them out.

EXTEND YOUR LEARNING

BOOKS

Benoit, Peter, Kevin Cunningham. *The Wampanoag (A True Book: American Indians)*. Children's Press, New York, 2011.

Harjo, Suzan Shown. *Nation to Nation: Treaties Between the United States & American Indian Nations*. National Museum of the American Indian, Washington, D.C., 2014.

Loh-Hagan, Virgina. *Stand Up, Speak Out: Indigenous Rights*. 45th Parallel Press, Ann Arbor, MI, 2022.

O'Brien, Cynthia. *Encyclopedia of American Indian History and Culture: Stories, Timelines, Maps and More*. National Geographic Kids, Boone, IA, 2019.

WEBSITES

With an adult, learn more online with these suggested searches.

"Iroquois (Native American people)," Britannica Kids.

"National Museum of the American Indian," Smithsonian.

"The Haudenosaunee Confederacy and the Constitution," Library of Congress Blogs.

GLOSSARY

allies (A-lies) supporters of a cause

Articles of Confederation (AHR-ti-kuls UHV kuhn-fe-duh-RAY-shuhn) the first constitution of the United States that created a "league of friendship" between 13 independent states with no required obligations between them

checks and balances (CHEKS uhnd BA-luhns) a system that distributes power and control

confederacy (kUHn-FE-druh-see) parties or states that unite and work together

Connecticut Compromise (kuh-NE-tih-kuht KAHM-pruh-miez) an agreement over division of representation in the two houses of the United States Congress

delegates (DE-li-guht) representatives of a larger group

Haudenosaunee (hoe-dee-no-SHOW-nee) powerful confederacy of six Indigenous nations of the northeast, including the Mohawk, Seneca, Onondaga, Oneida, Cayuga, and Tuscarora

impeached (im-PEECHT) removed from power

matrilineal (ma-truh-LIN-nee-uhl) traced through a mother's relations

ratified (RA-tuh-fied) officially approved and adopted

seven generations (SE-vuhn je-nuh-RAY-shuhns) the concept of making decisions today that would even benefit people seven generations in the future

sovereign (SAH-vruhn) independent

Treaty of Lancaster (TREE-tee UHV LAN-kuh-stuhr) a treaty with the Haudenosaunee and other Indigenous nations and the British government in 1744 that attempted to establish territory lines around Shenandoah Valley in Virginia

wampum belts (WAHM-puhm BELTS) lengths of woven, polished shells that symbolize a treaty, oath, or position of responsibility

INDEX